Beautiful Birds

BLUE JAYS

By Kristen Rajczak Nelson

Gareth Stevens
PUBLISHING

Please visit our website, www.garethstevens.com. For a free color catalog of all our high-quality books, call toll free 1-800-542-2595 or fax 1-877-542-2596.

Library of Congress Cataloging-in-Publication Data

Names: Rajczak Nelson, Kristen, author.
Title: Blue jays / Kristen Rajczak Nelson.
Description: New York : Gareth Stevens Publishing, [2023] | Series: Beautiful birds | Includes index.
Identifiers: LCCN 2021035971 (print) | LCCN 2021035972 (ebook) | ISBN 9781538275122 (set) | ISBN 9781538275139 (library binding) | ISBN 9781538275115 (paperback) | ISBN 9781538275146 (ebook)
Subjects: LCSH: Blue jay–Juvenile literature.
Classification: LCC QL696.P2367 R35 2023 (print) | LCC QL696.P2367 (ebook) | DDC 598.8/64–dc23
LC record available at https://lccn.loc.gov/2021035971
LC ebook record available at https://lccn.loc.gov/2021035972

First Edition

Published in 2023 by
Gareth Stevens Publishing
29 East 21st Street
New York, NY 10010

Editor: Kristen Nelson
Designer: Andrea Davison-Bartolotta

Photo credits: Cover, p. 5 FotoRequest/Shutterstock.com; p. 1 Tom Reichner/Shutterstock.com; pp. 7, 24 (crest) RT Images/Shutterstock.com; pp. 9, 24 (bill) karl umbriaco/Shutterstock.com; p. 11 Diane079F/Shutterstock.com; p. 13 Al Mueller/Shutterstock.com; p. 15 Noah Wegryn/Shutterstock.com; pp. 17, 24 (nest) Bruce MacQueen/Shutterstock.com; p. 19 David Tran Photo/Shutterstock.com; p. 21 Mastering_Microstock/Shutterstock.com; p. 23 Cytis77/Shutterstock.com.

Printed in the United States of America

CPSIA compliance information: Batch #CSGS23: For further information contact Gareth Stevens, New York, New York at 1-800-542-2595.

Contents

Blue jays are birds.
They are blue and gray.

Their head has feathers.
These are a crest.

They have black bills.

Blue jays live in forests.

They make noises.
These are calls.
One sounds like a bell!

They eat acorns, nuts,
and seeds.
They eat grasshoppers
and beetles.

Blue jays build nests.
They lay eggs.

Eggs can be blue,
green, or yellow.
They can have spots!

Babies come out of the eggs. They do not have many feathers.

Their parents feed them.

Words to Know

bill

crest

nest

Index